The Pirate's HANDBOOK

For Anna and Sophie

PUFFIN BOOKS
Published by the Penguin Group
Penguin Putnam Inc., 375 Hudson Street, New York, New York 10014, U.S.A.
Penguin Books Ltd, 27 Wrights Lane, London W8 5TZ, England
Penguin Books Australia Ltd, Ringwood, Victoria, Australia
Penguin Books Canada Ltd, 10 Alcorn Avenue, Toronto, Ontario, Canada M4V 3B2
Penguin Books (N.Z.) Ltd, 182-190 Wairau Road, Auckland 10, New Zealand

Penguin Books Ltd, Registered Offices: Harmondsworth, Middlesex, England

First published in the United States of America by Cobblehill Books,
an affiliate of Dutton Children's Books, a division of Penguin USA Inc., 1995
Published in Puffin Books, 1998

1 3 5 7 9 10 8 6 4 2

Conceived and produced by Breslich & Foss, London
Project editor: Catriona Woodburn
Designed by: Roger Daniels
Additional artwork and original projects: Tony Garrett
Photography: Nigel Bradley and Carl Adamson

THE LIBRARY OF CONGRESS HAS CATALOGED THE COBBLEHILL EDITION AS FOLLOWS:
Lincoln, Margarette.
The pirate's handbook/Margarette Lincoln.
p. cm.
ISBN 0-525-65209-4
1. Pirates—Juvenile literature. 2. Handicraft—Juvenile literature. [1. Pirates. 2. Handicraft.] I. Title.
G535.L55 1995 910.45—dc20 94-46512 CIP AC

Puffin Books ISBN 0-14-055988-4

Printed in China

PICTURE CREDITS

Unless otherwise stated, illustrations are from the collection of **John Falconer**.
Breslich and Foss are also grateful to the following individuals and institutions
for permission to reproduce illustrations – **The National Maritime Museum:**
Endpapers, British sailors boarding an Algerine pirate ship; p.5, Auguste-François
Biard's engraving of pirates dressed as women luring an unsuspecting ship; p.7
(top), original ship's biscuit; p.13, *The Point of Honor*, Cruickshank's engraving
of a flogging; p.13, cat-o'-nine-tails; p.16, capture of a pirate schooner; p.16
(top right), astrolabe; p.16 (right, center and bottom), details of Barbary galleys;
p.21, flintlock pistol of c.1730; p.24, hanging at execution dock; p.27, Atkinson's
painting, *Heaving the Lead*; p.28, Gheeraerts' painting of Sir Francis Drake.
Delaware Art Museum, Howard Pyle Collection: p.9, *Extorting Tribute from the
Citizens*; p.11, *Marooned*; p.22, *So the Treasure Was Divided*. **Peter Marsden:** p.22,
detail of pieces of eight. **Dover Press:** p.27 (right), woodcut by Thomas Bewick.

The Pirate's HANDBOOK

Margarette Lincoln

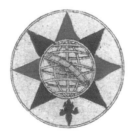

A Puffin Unicorn

Clothing and Disguises

Pirates did not wear a uniform. Most were poor men, and would simply set sail wearing the most seaworthy of their own clothes. However, when privateers turned to piracy, or pirates captured a naval ship, pieces of official naval uniform inevitably ended up in the pirate's wardrobe.

SOME LEADING PIRATE LOOKS THROUGH THE AGES

The Muslim Corsair (Sixteenth Century)

Fashion's strongest influence in the Mediterranean came from North Africa, with the hippest pirates there sporting Aladdin-style harem pants. Short jackets and round-necked shirts were detailed with rich embroidery; trousers were topped with a colorful cummerbund; and the turban, worn by all Muslim men, was a key feature.

The Buccaneer (Seventeenth Century)

The style of the European Cavaliers is the look associated with the buccaneer of the West Indies. A full-skirted jacket was worn, belted, over either knee-length breeches, trousers or stockings. The true buccaneer's footwear was a pair of bucket-topped boots; while heads were topped with brimmed hats, with colored feathers.

Pirate Power-dressing in East and West Africa (Early Eighteenth Century)

For the privateer turned pirate, plundering the Guinea coast or the seas around Madagascar, dress was more elaborate. Frock coats were typically worn with breeches, gartered stockings and square-toed, buckled shoes; hats had developed into the stately, three-cornered 'tricorne'; while gauntlets and deeply-cuffed sleeves presented an altogether more dashing image.

A Pirate from the Philippines (Nineteenth Century)

Markedly simpler, this outfit of a South China Seas pirate consisted of a cap-sleeved tunic over a skirt. A shawl was wound around the waist and hips (as a sword holster); and for the head, a large handkerchief or scarf was secured around the chin by another (as in cases of toothache!).

DRESSED TO KILL!
Creating your Classic Pirate Look

This is timeless pirate clothing and with these items in your wardrobe you can be sure to look the part at all piratical occasions, whether you're up the rigging or at the captain's table.

Make-up Tips
- A patch on the eye is a bold move. If you have already lost an eye in battle it suggests you are to be taken seriously.
- The hooped gold earring is one of the recognized symbols of piratehood.

Long shirt, or coat, or jacket
Without this item you're sunk.

Knee-length breeches
Those with the look of velvet are particularly classy, but not all pirates can run to such luxury.

Long socks
If your breeches are not long enough, you need long socks to avoid bare kneecaps.

Buckled shoes
Useful for walking the plank, dancing hornpipes, and showing off.

Soft, brimmed hat
To keep head warm.
(Hat feathers are optional, but strongly advised.)

Bandeau
This is just a fancy term for a headband. With or without a hat this gives credibility.

Neckerchief
For a flourish.

Long, bright scarf for a waist sash
Vital for holding up breeches, and as a weapons' holster.

Ribbon-ties as garters
Be as flamboyant as you dare. For the ultimate in color co-ordination, match ties to your headband and waist sash.

Optional extras:
gloves, waistcoat, gold accessories.

MAKING YOUR PIRATE SHOE BUCKLES

What you will need:

- cardboard [at least 15 × 15 cm (6 × 6 in.)]
- ruler
- felt-tip pen
- craft knife (TAKE CARE)
- aluminum foil
- pencil
- ribbon [approx. 2.5 cm (1 in.) wide and 102 cm (40 in.) long]
- paperclips or bobby pins.

1 Draw two rectangles on your cardboard, each 6.5 × 4 cm (2½ × 1½ in.) and cut them out. On the two longest sides, draw a line 1 cm (⅜ in.) from the edge, and on the two shorter sides, draw a line 1.5 cm (⅝ in.) from the edge. In the very center draw a band 1.5 cm (⅝ in.) wide.

2 To make the holes for threading ribbon through, cut out the two smaller rectangles you have drawn on each buckle.

3 Take pieces of aluminum foil and wrap them around your cardboard buckle. Cover the center strip. Using a pencil with a rounded point, mark a design onto the foil – taking care not to pierce it.

4 From underneath the buckle, thread the ends of ribbon up through the holes. Knot the ribbon on top and tie a large bow. Using a paperclip or bobby pin, attach the ribbon under the buckle to the shoelaces of your shoes.

If your shoes are without laces, you could clip your bows directly onto your shoes, or alternatively stick them on using double-sided tape.

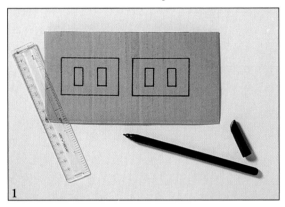

THE MAKE-UP SECRETS OF A PIRATE SUPER MODEL

Blackbeard terrorized the east coast of America at the beginning of the 18th century. He terrified people with his long black beard which he braided, tied with ribbons, and then tucked behind his ears. He would also light lengths of cord and leave them to smolder gently in his hatband.

Blackbeard, who struck terror into the hearts of all those who looked on him.

WHAT THE BEST-DRESSED WOMEN WORE

There were not a great many women pirates, but some were extremely powerful. Ching Shih had a pirate community of 80,000 under her command. Like Anne Bonny and Mary Read, who hid the fact that they were women, Ching Shih's clothing would have differed little from that of the male crew.

Anne Bonny, who dressed as a man to join "Calico" Jack's ship.

AND THE BEST-DRESSED MEN...

Bartholomew Roberts (Black Bart) was a lover of finery. At his death, he was fighting dressed in a crimson waistcoat and breeches, and a hat with a red feather. Round his neck was a gold chain with a diamond cross, and over his shoulders were two pairs of pistols in a silk sling. For a burial his crew threw him overboard in all his finery.

Black Bart.

PIRATES IN DISGUISE

After capturing two French ships, Howell Davis forced the crews to dress as pirates, and hoisted tarpaulins as sails. In this way he led passing ships to think he had a three-strong pirate flotilla and so persuaded them to surrender in the belief that they were outnumbered.

In this nineteenth-century engraving, pirates dressed up as women trick a passing ship into believing they are in need of assistance.

Provisions

If pirates were blown off course, or failed to take any ships, then they could easily run out of food and get very, very hungry. Pirates rarely ate a healthy diet, and without the vitamin C to be found in fresh fruit and vegetables they were likely to catch a disease called scurvy.

PIRATES' COOKERY SPOT

Salmagundi was a favorite pirate meal when food was plentiful. The pirate Bartholomew Roberts ate it for breakfast on the day that he died, when trying to avoid capture by a British warship in 1722. Perhaps he ate a bit too much and couldn't get away!
Here's how to make it:

Salmagundi: A light snack for a hungry pirate

INGREDIENTS:

Meats: 1 turtle, 1 fish, 1 chicken, 1 pig, 1 cow, 1 duck, 1 pigeon.

Marinade: Red wine, spices.

Accompaniments: Cabbage, pickled herring, anchovies, mangoes, onions, grapes, eggs (hard-boiled), pickled vegetables.

Seasonings: Garlic, salt, pepper, mustard seed, oil, vinegar.

For this spicy West Indian dish, first roast all the meats. Cut into chunks and marinate for several hours in spiced red wine. Remove, and mix with all remaining ingredients, having first chopped them into bite-sized pieces. Season to taste.

Bartholomew Roberts and his men enjoying wining and dining on shore.

LOTIONS AND POTIONS

When pirates seized a ship they often made straight for its medicine chest! This was a prized item of plunder, for pirates that were unwell were sometimes more worried about disease and injury than treasure. In the Tropics pirates risked fevers, and in stormy weather they caught colds from being in wet clothes for days.

DELICIOUS ALTERNATIVES FOR PIRATES FACING HARD TIMES

The pirate Basil Ringrose and his crew, active in the Caribbean in the 1680s, fell upon hard times and had to eat monkeys and snakes to survive. At Drake's Island, near San Francisco, other pirates caught and salted goats and turtles to last them while at sea. And in the China Seas in the 1800s, the crew of the female pirate Ching Shih "lived three weeks on caterpillars boiled in rice." They were so hungry that they were also forced to breed rats to eat – which were then considered a great delicacy.

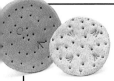

SHIP'S BISCUIT

Bread did not keep long at sea, so instead pirates ate plain biscuits, made of flour and very little water. Shaped into flat cakes, they were baked very slowly and then packed for storage in canvas bags. They quickly became infested with black-headed weevils, which had to be taken out before the biscuits could be eaten. For a tastier version for today's seafarers, try this scrumptious biscuit recipe:

INGREDIENTS:
8 oz (225 g) plain flour
2½ teaspoons baking powder
1 teaspoon salt
2 teaspoons sugar
4 oz (110 g) butter
2 fl oz (55 ml) milk

1 Sift the dry ingredients together into a mixing bowl. Using your fingertips, work the butter well into the mixture.

2 Stir in just enough milk to make a smooth, soft dough – not too sticky to be handled. Turn out onto a lightly-floured work surface and knead gently for about a minute.

3 Roll the dough out with a lightly-floured rolling pin, to between a ½ and 1 cm (¼ - ½ in.) thick.

4 Use a round cutter (or the floured top of a glass) to cut out your biscuits. Arrange on a buttered baking sheet.

5 Bake at 450°F/250°C for 12-15 minutes, or until lightly browned and done. Serve with butter and jam.

HAVE YOU GOT SCURVY?

Do this simple quiz to discover if you must see a doctor and be bled by leeches at the next port.

Do you have any of the following?

Sore gums	(Score A)
Rumbling stomach	(Score B)
Itchy feet	(Score C)

Which of the following have you noticed?

Dirt on your shirt	(Score B)
Lost your sea legs	(Score C)
Big red blotches under the skin	(Score A)

Which of the following do you feel when you wake in the morning?

Extremely fed-up	(Score C)
Extremely poorly	(Score A)
Extremely hungry	(Score B)

How to Discover if you have Scurvy:

MOSTLY C'S: You are a frustrated pirate who has spent too much time on dry land.

CURE: Get to sea with haste.

MOSTLY B'S: You are a starving pirate who has run out of clean clothes.

CURE: Make some filling ship's biscuits and eat them while soaking in the bathtub.

ENTIRELY A'S: You are a sickly pirate, and probably have scurvy. (NB If you develop these symptoms on land, put on your sea boots and get to the doc quick.)

CURE: Stop at the next port for some oranges and green beans. Indulge.

Having a Good Time

Pirates were happiest when they had plenty of money to spend and were enjoying themselves on dry land. Their life at sea was very hard, but sometimes there was fun to be had onboard ship too. Singing, for example, helped with repetitive work as well as providing entertainment.

MOCK COURTS

18th-century pirates knew that, if caught, they would be tried before a court of law and probably sentenced to death. To cheer themselves up, they often held mock trials. In these, they could dress up as the judge, jury, and even the poor pirate who had been caught, and make fun of the whole thing.

. . . AND A BOTTLE OF RUM

Often pirates wasted all their money when they reached land, on drinking and gambling. The idea that most pirates buried their treasure on desert islands is probably untrue, for almost all of them would have spent everything they had on shore. Port Royal, in Jamaica, was a favorite spot amongst pirates, and it gained a reputation as the wickedest city in the world. It had so many taverns that there was one for every 150 people. When the city was devastated by an earthquake in 1692, many said it was God's punishment on the place.

In 1722, on an uninhabited island off the coast of Cuba, Thomas Anstis' crew whiled away months by dancing and holding mock courts, while they waited to hear if they had been granted an official pardon for piracy.

Pirates demanding treasure from the people of the town.

GOING ASHORE

Pirates sometimes plundered the cities they passed through when they went ashore, but usually when pirates reached land they came to stock-up on food and medicines, make repairs to their ships, and enjoy themselves. Blackbeard frequently got married! Some say he had fourteen wives in different ports.

REPAIRING SHIPS

Wooden ships had to be carefully maintained to keep them seaworthy. Every so often the ship had to be "careened" – put onto its side so that weed and barnacles could be scraped off the bottom. Weed slowed ships down, and pirate ships had to be fast in case they were chased. Pirates found quiet inlets to repair their ships.

CODE OF CONDUCT

What follows is the strict and solemn code of the crew of the good ship

....

— RULE 1 —

Everyone must obey the commands of the captain.

— RULE 2 —

Everyone shall have a share of any treasure, but for every piece of gold a member of the crew is given, the captain will be given one and a half.

— RULE 3 —

If anyone steals or gambles, they will be marooned, with only a bottle of water, and a pistol.

— RULE 4 —

Anyone who encourages a new pirate to join the crew without everyone else's agreement will suffer whatever punishment the captain and the crew think fit.

— RULE 5 —

Anyone that strikes another crew member while these rules are in force, shall receive 39 lashes with the whip.

— RULE 6 —

Anyone that raises their weapon when not in battle, or leaves a lighted candle unguarded, will suffer the same punishment as in Rule 5.

— RULE 7 —

Anyone that doesn't keep their weapons clean, or in any other ways is not prepared for action, will not receive their share of any treasure, and will suffer what further punishment the captain and the crew think fit.

— RULE 8 —

If anyone loses a finger or a toe in a battle, they shall be given 400 pieces of eight, and if they lose an arm or a leg, they shall have 800 pieces.

Signed..

In Witness..

Loyal sea rovers both

Codes of Conduct

Most pirates were originally seamen by trade. Many hated naval discipline, and banded together instead in pirate gangs. Although they were desperate men, they had their own rules about how to behave and would punish those that broke them.

HONOR AMONGST THIEVES

Onboard the ship *Revenge*, the pirate John Phillips and his men drew up a set of rules for how their pirate crew should behave. Pirates had to swear upon the bible or a hatchet to keep to them, and another pirate signed them in witness.

"I shall make you governor of the next desert island we see!"
This painting, entitled Marooned, *by Howard Pyle, shows the lot of the abandoned pirate.*

BREAKING THE RULES

If a pirate broke the pirate code, or committed some other serious offense, he could be marooned on a desert island. His shipmates would leave him on the beach with just a bottle of water and some shot for his gun. Most pirates who were punished in this way died a slow death from

WRITING A CODE OF CONDUCT
(For Keeping in a Safe Place)

What you will need:
- tracing paper
- pencil
- plain paper

Trace the border from the version of John Phillips' code of conduct, opposite, onto your page.

Next, you need to think about your own rules: What time must

lights out in the cabins be? What forfeit or punishment will be carried out if this is broken? Is there a ceremony for swearing in new pirate recruits? Write your rules down on your document.

Each crew member will need his own copy of the rules – signed by himself, and another crew member in witness.

exposure to heat and cold, and from hunger and thirst. Pirate Edward England was marooned by his crew for being too kind-hearted toward prisoners. He managed to build a small boat, and sailed in it to Madagascar where, apparently, he died in poverty.

ROBINSON CRUSOE

Daniel Defoe's *Robinson Crusoe* is a novel about a man shipwrecked on a desert island. The story, published in 1719, is said to have been inspired by Alexander Selkirk, a Scottish sailor who was put ashore on the island of Juan Fernandez (off the coast of Chile) by the adventurer and pirate William Dampier. Selkirk spent four and a half lonely years on this island until he was rescued — by that time he looked like a wild man.

The Island of Juan Fernandez, where Alexander Selkirk was marooned.

An eighteenth-century illustration for Robinson Crusoe.

Flogging (being lashed with a whip) was a common punishment for pirates that broke the code of conduct of their ship. The cat-o'-nine-tails, often just known as "the cat," was a nine-thonged whip that was regularly used.

THE PIRATE CAPTAIN

The captain was the most important person onboard ship, but he was elected by the crew and they could get rid of him too. Captains were obeyed in battle, but otherwise important decisions were taken by a show of hands from the whole crew.

SHARING BOOTY

Plunder was divided amongst pirates in agreed proportions by the quartermaster. Sometimes there was a special scribe onboard, whose job it was to make a list of the goods and prisoners captured (so that the money made from them could be shared out later).

OFFICIALLY APPROVED PIRACY

Piracy as Big Business

Governments sometimes gave captains of armed merchant ships a written commission or "letter of marque," authorizing them to capture the merchant ships of an enemy nation. These captains were called privateers — as were their ships — and they kept a share of any profits. Some authorities even organized "prize courts," for the sale and disposal of captured ships and their cargoes.

Some privateers abused their commission and captured merchant ships in peacetime too, taking the plunder all for themselves. The line between a privateer and a pirate was often a fine one.

Crusading Pirates

Religious reasons also provided an excuse for pirates to plunder ships. In the 16th century, the Christian Knights of St. John, based in Malta (in the Mediterranean), gave official licenses for Christian privateers to attack Islamic ships.

PARDONS

From time to time, governments became so concerned about the presence of pirates on the seas that they offered official pardons to them if they agreed to give themselves up. In 1698 a royal proclamation declared a general pardon to all the pirates in the seas around Madagascar. John Ward, however, one of the most feared corsair captains in the Mediterranean, had his refused. As a result he converted to Islam, adopting the name Yusuf Rais, and remained under the protection of the Dey of Tunis.

Charts, Coastlines and Hideaways

At the turn of the 18th century, much of the world was unexplored, and those charts which did exist were carefully guarded. Some pirates were able to capture charts, others – such as the brilliant buccaneer Basil Ringrose – were clever enough to make their own.

ALL MAPPED OUT

A nation which hoped to increase its trade or conquer new territory needed accurate maps. Some pirates helped to spread knowledge of the world because they wrote accounts of their piratical voyages and included sketch maps of coastlines.

Charts were used by pirates themselves to work out the likely routes taken by treasure ships and to spot towns for plundering. It was also important that pirates should know of places to shelter when their ships needed repairing.

A chart by Baptista Boazio, illustrating the coastline of Hispaniola (now Haiti and the Dominican Republic).

PIRATE BASES

Madagascar
A Base in the Indian Ocean
Pirates sometimes took over whole islands. Madagascar was a base from which pirates captured luxury goods from the East, such as silks and spices.

The pirate Henry Avery became known as "King of Madagascar." In 1695 his fleet seized the *Gang-i-Sawai*, the largest ship owned by the Great Mogul of India. This ship was packed with treasure worth thousands and thousands of dollars. Avery was never captured.

"King of Madagascar."

New Providence
A Pirate Paradise in the Bahamas
Around 1700, pirates found the perfect hideout in the island of New Providence. It had fresh water and lots of fruit; and the outlying reefs were full of fish, lobsters, and turtles. There was no law on the island and pirates were able to laze away their days. There was a saying that when a pirate slept, he did not dream that he had died and gone to heaven, he dreamed that he had once again anchored in New Providence.

MAKING A TREASURE MAP

What you will need:
- medium-weight plain paper
- colored pencils or waterproof pens
- a used, slightly damp teabag
- ribbon
- colored, bakeable modeling clay
- old or new coin(s), as big as possible

1 Draw a map of a desert island. Decide where your camp is. Where do you go to fish for food? Where are the swampy places? And where would you bury any treasure? Put on as many sites as you like.

2 Make your map look old. Bend the corners and tear them a little. Use the teabag (not too damp) to wipe over the drawing. Leave to dry.

3 You could roll up the map, tie ribbon around the outside, and add a seal. Seals can be made from pressing a coin into modeling clay. Remove the coin and bake the clay for about 20 minutes. Cut a small

"V" out of one end of the ribbon and stick the seal close to the other end. Alternatively, you could cut a line at the bottom of your map, and thread your ribbon through this, with the seal hanging at the front.

Bias Bay

A Famous Hideout (East of Hong Kong) in the China Seas

In the 19th century, the Chinese pirate Chui Apoo chose Bias Bay as his headquarters. There were dockyards there, for vessels to be built and repaired. Chui Apoo's power came to an end in 1849, but the bay remained a hideout for sea robbers until the 1930s. Nowadays pirates still operate from hidden inlets and little-known islands in the seas of Southeast Asia.

An attack on Chui Apoo's pirate fleet by a British man-of-war.

Pirate Ships

Pirates around the world used different kinds of ships, but all pirates needed ships that were fast and powerful. They preferred ships with as shallow a depth below the water as possible, so that they could navigate in coastal waters and hide in secluded coves.

SCHOONER

The two-masted schooner was a favorite with pirates in North American waters. These ships were fast and easily maneuvered. They had a shallow draught (depth below the waterline), but were big enough to carry many guns and quite a large crew.

Capture of a pirate schooner.

GALLEYS

The Barbary corsairs, operating in the Mediterranean in the 17th and 18th centuries, used oar-powered galleys to prey on merchant

A 17th-century Barbary galley. It carries one large gun but the ram was its main weapon.

ships. These long, extremely narrow ships had a sail, but when in action they were rowed and could then reach fast speeds. Each oar was manned by up to six slaves, chained to benches. The aim of the corsairs was to ram the enemy ship, board her and defeat the crew in hand-to-hand fighting. These galleys were really only suited to the Mediterranean, where conditions were calmer.

CAPTAIN DEVIL'S ROUND SHIP

Simon Danziger, nicknamed Captain Devil, was a Dutchman who joined the Barbary corsairs in the 1600s. He introduced the "round ship," a strong, three-masted sailing ship first used in northern waters, to the corsairs in the Mediterranean. Once they could sail it, they were able to extend their raids into the much rougher waters of the Atlantic.

GETTING TO KNOW THE ROPES

All pirates had to have the skills of sailors, and for pirates on sailing ships this included knowing about knots! Take some rope and practice these:

THE REEF KNOT: Used for tying together pieces of rope.

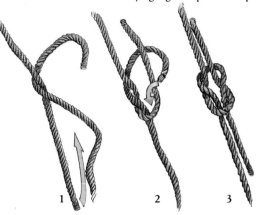

1   2   3

1. Cross the two ropes, as shown, and then pull the end of one rope back to form a loop. 2. Feed the free end of the other rope through the loop. 3. Pull tight.

THE BOWLINE: Used whenever you need a loop.

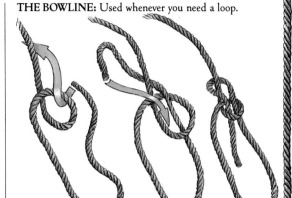

1   2   3

1. Make a loop. Feed the free end through. 2. Take the free end behind the rope, around it, and back through the loop. 3. Pull tight.

CAPTURED SHIPS

Pirates in the Atlantic often took over captured merchant ships, and altered them to suit their purpose. They might reduce the height of a ship to increase her speed, and cut more gunports so that they could use more cannon. These changes also helped to hide the identity of a captured ship.

THE JUNK

The traditional vessel in Chinese waters was the flat-bottomed "junk," which had three masts and sails held together with bamboo rods. The largest junks had twelve guns and carried rowing boats, used for raiding coastal villages or boarding other ships.

A South China trading junk.

CAPTAIN KIDD'S SHIP

Captain William Kidd was given a specially designed ship in order to carry out a privateering expedition licensed by the King. The *Adventure Galley* could reach good speeds using sails, but could also be rowed when in a calm. With two or three pirates at each of her 42 oars, she could move quite quickly, despite having 32 heavy cannon onboard.

Captain Kidd's commission was to attack French merchant ships and also to seize pirates. However, when his expedition went wrong he turned to piracy himself.

Flags

Traditionally, a ship flies the flag of the country that owns her, but not pirate ships. Sometimes pirates deceived passing vessels by flying the flag of a friendly country, but often they flew their own flags – the most famous of which was the skull and crossbones of The Jolly Roger.

FALSE COLORS

Pirate ships often carried onboard the flags of several countries, and flew whichever one they thought would help them get close to their victim without suspicion. This was known as flying "false colors." The officially commissioned privateers, however, when seizing enemy merchant ships in wartime, flew the flag of the country that had hired them.

THE LANGUAGE OF FLAGS

Your time is running out

Death

Torment

A violent death awaits you

A slow, painful death awaits you

We are ready to kill you

FLAGS, WHITE AND RED

Pirates deliberately built-up a reputation for cruelty and violence. They used flags to frighten passing ships, hoping that they would surrender without too much of a fight. When giving chase, pirates often flew a white flag. If the merchant ship refused to slow down, the pirates hoisted a red flag. The red flag signified blood. The message it sent to the resisting ship was that once the pirates boarded, no one would be spared.

THE JOLLY ROGER

The skull and crossbones flag is the most famous symbol of pirate terror. The first Jolly Roger appeared around 1700 when the pirate Emmanuel Wynne hoisted one in the Caribbean. The flag quickly caught on and other pirates designed their own versions. The Jolly Roger was flown when pirates were close to their victims and wanted to frighten them badly. No one knows the origin of the name. It may have come from the French *joli rouge* (pretty red), a joking description of the blood-red flag flown by earlier pirates. The name Old Roger was given to the flag owned by pirates later hanged on Rhode Island, in 1723.

HOIST A PIRATE FLAG

Sir Francis Drake flew the flag of St. George when capturing Spanish ships in the name of Queen Elizabeth I of England. Make a flag to your own design. Decide what meaning your symbols will have to those you capture.

What you will need:

- round wooden rod [minimum 60 cm (24 in.) in length and 9 mm (⅜ in.) in diameter]
- 1 picture-hanging hoop screw or a ring-pull from a soft-drink can
- masking tape
- black material or black plastic
- scissors
- string (double the length of your rod)
- plain white paper
- pencil
- fluorescent paint or pen
- glue

1 Screw the hoop screw into the wooden rod, about 2 cm (¾ in.) from one end, or use a ring-pull from a soft-drink can, attached firmly to the side of the rod with masking tape.

2 Cut a rectangle out of black material or plastic [approx. 40 × 35 cm (16 × 40 in.)]. Glue one of the shorter edges around the middle of the length of string so it is stuck securely.

3 On paper, draw your design for a flag – a skull perhaps, or one of the symbols on page 18. Color it (fluorescent colors are great) and cut it out. Glue it to your black flag.

4 Thread the string above the flag down through the screw/ring-pull and tie it to the other end of the string. Hoist the flag. Wrap the string around the pole to keep it secured.

The flags of Bartholomew Roberts' pirate ships.

BLACK BART'S OWN DESIGN

Bartholomew Roberts was so angry with the governors of Martinique and Barbados for continually trying to capture him, that he created a special flag to make them fear for their lives. The flag showed a figure of himself standing on two skulls. Under them were the letters ABH and AMH, meaning A Barbadian's Head and A Martinican's Head. Around 1720, Roberts managed to carry out part of his threat: he caught the governor of Martinique and hung him from the mast.

The Attack

Throughout history, pirates of all nations have relied heavily on speed and surprise when making an attack. In the past, pirates sometimes achieved surprise by trickery. They flew the flag of a friendly nation, or posed as cargo vessels or harmless passenger ships.

BOARDING

When the pirate ship was right behind its victim (avoiding the guns positioned along the side of a ship), agile pirates would jam the victim's rudder with wooden wedges so that she couldn't be steered. They swung hooked ropes into the merchant ship and then swarmed up them, barefooted for a surer grip and armed to the teeth.

Pirates also made use of homemade weapons. They made hand grenades by filling old wine bottles with gunpowder, and created smoke screens by setting fire to foul-smelling, yellow sulphur.

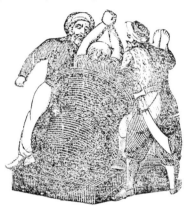

A cruel punishment for a captured crew member.

DEFENDING A SHIP

Merchant seamen under attack did what they could to stop pirates from boarding their ship. They greased the decks, or scattered dried peas or broken bottles. They knew, however, that if they put up a strong fight and lost, the pirates would show little mercy. Terrible tales were told of what pirates did to captured crew. Stede Bonnet made his prisoners walk the plank (to death by drowning), while Edward Low cut the ears off the master of one ship, and made him eat them himself with pepper and salt.

A flintlock pistol of c.1730.

PIRATE WEAPONS

18th-century pirates used pistols, daggers, and cutlasses. These weapons were suited to close fighting. Cannon were used when firing on a ship, but Antonio Fuët, known as Captain Moidore, ran out of cannonballs and was

MAKE A PIRATE'S SWORD

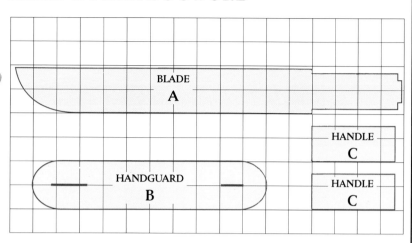

BLADE
A

HANDLE
C

HANDGUARD
B

HANDLE
C

What you will need:
- cardboard
  [50 × 20 cm (20 × 8 in.)]
- scissors
- ribbon [approx. 20 cm (8 in.)]
- glue
- aluminum foil

On cardboard, draw a grid four times as big as the one shown. One square should equal 2.5 cm (1 in.) on your drawing.

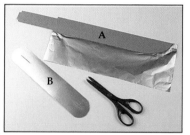

1 Draw parts A–C on your enlarged grid. Cut them out. Cut foil to cover both sides of the blade and one side of the handle. Glue the foil in place and cut around it to trim the edges.

2 Cut slits, as marked on the template, at each end of the handguard (B). Bend the handguard into an arch and push the sword handle through the slits, as shown.

3 Build up the thickness of the handgrip by sticking the cardboard rectangles (C) above and below the existing handle, directly under the handguard. Wrap ribbon around this thickened handgrip. Stick down or tuck in the end of the ribbon.

forced to use gold coins when firing on a Portuguese ship. Greedy surgeons are said to have used scalpels to remove the coins from the dead.

AT THE END OF THE DAY
Pirates might sink a captured ship, in order to get rid of evidence that could convict them. Otherwise it was added to the pirate fleet, with changes made to its structure and to its name.

When Captain Kidd captured the *Rupparell*, he had the name painted out and then changed it to *November*.

What would you call a ship?

Pirate Treasure

In Drake's time, pirates hunted ships bringing gold from South America. Later they sought ships from the East, laden with silks, jewels, and spices; and when the *Santo Rosario* was captured off San Francisco, the treasure included fine linen and 620 jars of wine and brandy.

PIECES OF EIGHT

Most seamen became pirates because they hoped to become rich, but pirate plunder was only valuable when exchanged for cash. Pirates were overjoyed if they captured a ship carrying money, not least because coins were more easily shared amongst the crew. In storybooks, pirates mostly seem to deal in pieces of eight. These were Spanish in origin, and worth about one dollar. Between the 17th and 19th centuries, they were accepted as currency almost worldwide.

HUMAN TREASURE

The Barbary corsairs, operating from the North African coast, found that more money could be made by taking prisoners hostage than by seeking rich cargoes. Prisoners were ransomed or sold as slaves (sometimes sent to row in galley ships).

Howard Pyle's painting So the Treasure Was Divided.

MAKING GOLDEN DUBLOONS AND
SILVER PIECES OF EIGHT

Pirates liked to enjoy themselves when they went ashore, and were not noted for their savings. Certainly very few of them held onto their money long enough to bury any of it.

What you will need:
- lids or pastry cutters to draw around to make small circles
- cardboard
- cork
- craft knife (TAKE CARE)
- scissors
- aluminum and gold foil
- pencil.

1 Draw around lids or pastry cutters onto the cardboard.

2 Cut the discs out. For smaller coins, carefully slice off pieces from a cork.

3 Cover all the pieces with silver or gold foil – with the shiny side facing out.

4 Draw designs on top, using a pencil. (Take care not to pierce through the foil.)

BURIED TREASURE

Most pirates did not bury their treasure and leave behind a map. Instead they squandered their loot on women, gambling, and drinking. Supposedly, Captain Kidd did bury his treasure on Gardiner's Island, New York, but he didn't live to reclaim it and it has never been found.

French pirate Olivier le Vasseur (alias The Buzzard), is also said to have buried a fortune. In 1721 he seized a Portuguese ship carrying gold and silver bars, chests of gold guineas, casks of diamonds, silks, and luxury goods worth a fortune. The Buzzard was captured alive in 1730. At his hanging he is said to have flung a roll of documents at the crowd with the challenge, "Find my treasure, who can!"

GUJERATI ROVERS

For hundreds of years, native pirates operated off the western coast of India. The Gujerati Rovers were reputed to be the most dangerous. Suspecting that their victims might swallow their most precious jewels, they made up a disgusting drink of tamarind mixed with sea water, which they forced them to swallow. The drink made the captives violently sick, so the pirates got their treasure after all.

Punishment

riginally, pirates who were convicted had little chance of escaping with their lives. In London, they were taken to "Execution Dock," where they were drowned. This gave way to hanging and other punishments, including flogging and branding on the forehead with a "P."

TAR AND CHAINS

Captain Kidd was hung at Execution Dock in 1701. The chaplain urged him to repent, but he was too drunk to listen. Kidd was an unlucky pirate, and bad fortune pursued him to the end. The rope broke and he had to be strung up a second time. His body was tarred to preserve it and then hung in chains at Tilbury Point in the Thames estuary. It hung there for years, swinging in the wind. Later pirates swore they would rather blow themselves to hell than be "hang'd up a sun-drying" like Captain Kidd.

Kidd's body, bound and hanging in an iron frame.

BLACKBEARD'S END

In addition to his terrifying appearance, Blackbeard increased his reputation for wickedness by shooting a member of his crew. After a particularly profitable seizure of ships, Blackbeard took an oath to be a law-abiding citizen, and was given a certificate of registration. When he returned to sea, he was careful to take this with him as proof of his pardon, although in practice he was soon up to his old tricks. Eventually he was caught in the shallows of Ocracoke Inlet, North Carolina, by

A pirate hanging at Execution Dock, about 1780. The figure wearing a long black gown is the chaplain.

Lieutenant Maynard in HMS *Pearl*. There followed one of the great battles of pirate history in which Blackbeard was killed. He did not die easily. When his corpse was examined, he was found to have 25 wounds, including five

Legend has it that Blackbeard's headless corpse, thrown into the Ocracoke, swam around Maynard's ship several times in defiance before sinking from sight.

pistol shots. Maynard was determined to make an example of the pirate. He cut off Blackbeard's head and tied it as a trophy to the yardarm of his ship.

A PICKLED HEAD

The pirate John Phillips was killed in 1724 when his men, many of whom he had forced to become pirates, rose up against him. The mutineers were led by Captain Haraden, whose fine new ship Phillips had just captured and taken over. Phillip's head was brought to Boston in pickled brine.

WOMEN PIRATES

Anne Bonny and Mary Read were caught in 1720 and taken to prison in Jamaica. Though found guilty, they both escaped the death sentence because they were pregnant. Sadly, Mary died of fever in prison before her child was born. Unlike these two, Massachusetts' famous pirate, Rachel Wall, was hanged. She was reputed to have attempted to tear out the tongue of a woman whose hat she had tried to steal.

Anne Bonny escaped being put to death because she was pregnant.

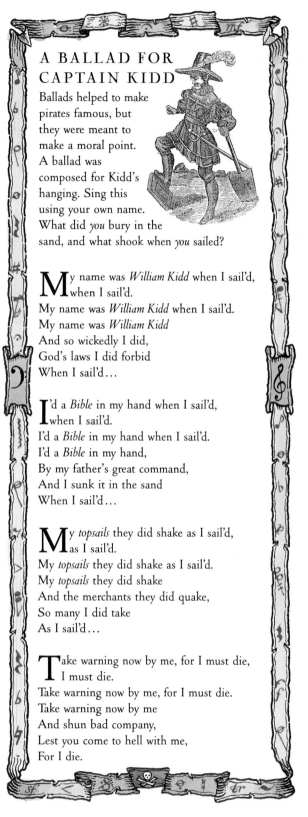

A BALLAD FOR CAPTAIN KIDD

Ballads helped to make pirates famous, but they were meant to make a moral point. A ballad was composed for Kidd's hanging. Sing this using your own name. What did *you* bury in the sand, and what shook when *you* sailed?

My name was *William Kidd* when I sail'd, when I sail'd.
My name was *William Kidd* when I sail'd.
My name was *William Kidd*
And so wickedly I did,
God's laws I did forbid
When I sail'd…

I'd a *Bible* in my hand when I sail'd, when I sail'd.
I'd a *Bible* in my hand when I sail'd.
I'd a *Bible* in my hand,
By my father's great command,
And I sunk it in the sand
When I sail'd…

My *topsails* they did shake as I sail'd, as I sail'd.
My *topsails* they did shake as I sail'd.
My *topsails* they did shake
And the merchants they did quake,
So many I did take
As I sail'd…

Take warning now by me, for I must die, I must die.
Take warning now by me, for I must die.
Take warning now by me
And shun bad company,
Lest you come to hell with me,
For I die.

Piratical Language

*S*eamen had a language of their own. Much of it came from the names given to different parts of the ship and rigging, which were rarely heard on land. Sailors looked down on those who knew nothing of life aboard, and enjoyed talking in terms that landlubbers couldn't understand.

To go on the account

This term was used by buccaneers to describe their life at sea. When someone asked them what their plans were, it sounded more respectable to say they were going to "go on the account" rather than "turn pirate."

Avast ye landlubbers!

"Avast" means Stop! or Stay!, and a "lubber" was a clumsy person; so a landlubber was someone who was as clumsy onboard ship as a person who had never been to sea. The phrase was used dismissively by pirates when calling out to those who were not sea rovers like themselves.

Davy Jones

This is the sailor's name for the sea devil who was supposed to rule the evil spirits of the deep. When ships sank, they were said to have gone to Davy Jones's Locker and so this became the seaman's phrase for death. David Jones was mate, and for a time captain, of a royal pirate ship called the *Roebuck*. His practice of sinking plundered ships during the early seventeenth century was perhaps the inspiration for the phrase.

Walking the plank

This cruel practice, made famous through pirate stories, involved forcing prisoners to walk down a plank into the sea and there, inevitably, to their death by drowning. It isn't known with what frequency this took place, but it is thought that it possibly originated with the capture of Romans by Greek pirates in the last 100 years BC. Greek pirates would pretend to their Roman captives that they felt guilty for what they had done and would beg for pardon. When the captives were convinced of their sincerity, the pirates would let down the ship's ladder and offer the Romans their freedom – before throwing them into the sea.

Swinging the lead

In coastal waters it was important for pirates to know the depth of the water and the nature of the seabed. To do this they used a rope, marked in fathoms, which had a lead weight at one end. It was called a lead line. The lead could be plugged with wax, which would pick up samples from the seabed – sand, gravel or mud – so that the sailor would know the nature of the seabed. Because the job of swinging the lead was thought to be an easy one, the phrase came to mean avoiding work, as in "he's swinging the lead."

To be keelhauled

This means to be told off harshly, and comes from the punishment of keelhauling. This was where a person was dragged by a rope from one side of a vessel to the other through the water under the keel.

Sea legs

A sailor gained his "sea legs" when he had been onboard ship long enough to become used to its rolling motion and not feel seasick. After months on a ship, a pirate walking on land would be noted for his swaying walk until he recovered his "land legs!"

Yellow Jack

This is the sailor's name for yellow fever. It was also the name given to the yellow flag that seamen were supposed to fly to warn other ships that there was illness onboard.

Take a caulk

To help keep a ship watertight, the gaps between the planking on deck were "caulked." This meant that they were filled with old rope and then sealed with tar. In hot weather a seaman who slept on deck might find his clothes marked with lines of the tar. Consequently, when a sailor slept on a ship's deck, he was said to "take a caulk." This is the likely origin of the expression, although it may be even simpler – that the caulked seams on deck are horizontal, as are sleeping seamen!

Shiver me timbers

When a wooden ship runs aground or suddenly hits a rock, her timbers shiver. So the expression "shiver me timbers" is one of surprise or shock.

Long clothes

These were the kind of clothes worn on land. Seamen had to wear loose trousers and short jackets that would not get in the way when they climbed up the rigging. Landsmen, in contrast, wore long coats, breeches, and stockings.

Tipping the black spot

Traditionally, when a pirate tipped someone the black spot, they were threatening them with death. In Robert Louis Stevenson's *Treasure Island,* the pirate Blind Pew leaves Captain Bill Bones a piece of paper with a black spot painted on one side of it, and on the other, the summons: "You have 'til ten tonight."

Pirate Types

A pirate is the name given to a sea robber. Throughout history pirates have been associated with different parts of the world, and in some places piracy is as common today as it ever was. Danger spots include the waters off West Africa, the Caribbean and the East Indies.

BUCCANEER

A buccaneer was the name given, originally, to those who hunted cattle and pigs on the island of Hispaniola (now Dominica and Haiti). When driven out by the Spanish, many turned to piracy. Thus the term came to refer to the pirates and privateers of the late 17th century who operated from bases in the West Indies, chiefly Port Royal, Jamaica, and the island of Tortuga off Hispaniola. Buccaneers had a reputation for hard drinking and extreme cruelty.

An original buccaneer of Hispaniola.

PRIVATEER

A privateer was authorized by his government to attack the ships of hostile nations. Between the 15th and 18th centuries, governments issued "letters of marque"

Sir Francis Drake.

to authorize this, and in theory this prevented privateers from being charged with piracy. However, many privateers took the law into their own hands and were really no more than pirates. Sir Francis Drake was authorized, in just this way, to prey on Spanish treasure ships bringing gold and silver from South America to Europe in the 1570s.

CORSAIR

This term covers both the Muslim and Christian privateers active in the Mediterranean from the 16th to the 19th centuries. The Barbary corsairs operated specifically from the North African states of Algiers, Tunis, Tripoli, and Morocco, and were authorized by their governments to attack the ships of Christian countries.

Ali Khoja, a Barbary corsair and ruler of Algiers.

The Maltese corsairs, on the other hand, were granted license by the Christian Knights of St. John to attack the Turks.

A ROGUES' GALLERY
The Low-down on some Famous Pirates

Name Henry Avery.
Alias Long Ben Avery, John Avery.
Born About 1653.
Birthplace Near Plymouth, England.
Worked Indian Ocean.
Career Went to sea as a boy. Drifted into piracy in his early forties when he mutinied and seized his captain's ship. In 1695 he was lucky enough to capture the largest ship belonging to the Great Mogul of India. Her cargo was worth thousands of pounds.
Ship *Fancy.*
Fate Story has it that he was unable to sell his plunder without being found out. Merchants in England cheated him of his loot, and he died in poverty.

Name Bartholomew Roberts.
Alias Black Bart.
Born About 1682.
Birthplace England.
Appearance Wore expensive clothes.
Worked West Africa, Brazilian coast, New England coast, West Indies.
Career Roberts captured 400 ships in less than four years.
Ships *Royal Rover. Royal Fortune.*
Fate Killed in battle with Navy warship in 1722. The crew were captured; 52 were hung.

Name Captain William Kidd.
Born About 1645.
Birthplace Scotland.
Appearance Wore a wig.
Worked Indian Ocean.
Career An ex-privateer in the West Indies, Kidd emigrated to New York where he made a good marriage. In 1695 he visited England on business and was persuaded to lead a privateering mission against troublesome pirates. But Kidd's crew were a bad lot and he turned pirate himself, partly to appease his men with loot. In an argument he killed one of his crew by throwing a bucket at his head.
Fate Found guilty of piracy and murder. Executed at Wapping, London, England, in 1701. His tarred body was hung in a metal frame as a warning.

Name Anne Bonny.
Birthplace Near Cork, Ireland.
Appearance Physically strong.
Worked West Indies.
Career The illegitimate daughter of a lawyer and his serving maid, she was taken by her parents to Carolina, North America, where her father bought a plantation. She married a seaman, and went to live in the Bahamas. There she fell in love with Jack Rackham and joined his pirate ship in male disguise.
Fate Captured with Rackham and Mary Read in 1720, but escaped hanging because pregnant.

Name Sir Henry Morgan.
Born 1635.
Birthplace Wales.
Appearance Long hair, plump, with a moustache and beard.
Worked West Indies.
Career Came from a good family of farmers, but wanted a more exciting life and turned to buccaneering. Sacked the city of Panama in 1671.
Ship *Satisfaction.*
Fate Became Deputy Governor of Jamaica. Died of dropsy in 1688.

Name Mary Read.
Birthplace London, England.
Appearance Handsome when dressed as a man. Noted for her modesty.
Worked West Indies.
Career Mary was brought up as a boy, after her elder half-brother died as a baby. This had meant that Mary's relations had helped pay for her keep. When Mary grew up she married a soldier, but he died. She joined the navy, but her ship was captured by pirates. She fell in love with a member of the crew who had been forced to join the pirates and fought a duel on his behalf. She killed her opponent.
Fate Captured with Anne Bonny. She escaped hanging because she was pregnant, but died in prison before her baby was born.

Name Edward Teach or Thatch.
Alias Blackbeard.
Birthplace Bristol, England.
Appearance Long black beard, braided with ribbons. Black clothing. Wore long sulphur matches under his hat brim, which were lit to frighten his victims.
Worked American coast from Newfoundland to Trinidad.
Career Ex-privateer who turned to piracy in 1716. In 1717 he terrorized the people of Charles Town, South Carolina, and captured all the ships they left in the harbor. His crew needed medicine so he held his prisoners to ransom and demanded a chest of medicines for their safe return. He got what he wanted.
Ship *Queen Anne's Revenge.*
Fate Killed in battle against naval warships in 1718.